Hannah and Rob's
Little Book of Viola Jokes

Robert Steadman is a composer of operas and symphonies to music for brass band and even radio jingles. He conducts and, once in a while, plays the tuba.

Hannah Borrill is a composer and violinist. She has written works for orchestra and scores for a variety of theatre productions. She also plays... viola!

Hannah and Rob's
Little Book of Viola Jokes

Robert Steadman & Hannah Borrill

Perfect Fifth Publications UK

Steadman, Robert and Borrill, Hannah

Hannah and Rob's Little Book of Viola Jokes

© 2018, Robert Steadman and Hannah Borrill.

All Rights Reserved.

ISBN-13:978-1724342614
ISBN-10:1724342614

ALL RIGHTS RESERVED.
This book contains material protected under International and Federal Copyright Laws and Treaties. Any unauthorized reprint or use of this material is prohibited. No part of this book may be reproduced or transmitted in any form or by photocopying, recording, or by any in formation storage and retrieval system without express written per mission from the author/publisher.

CONTENTS

A brief history of viola jokes - page 14

THE JOKES

Jokes about violas - page 21

Jokes about viola players - page 27

Jokes which might need a
little bit of musical knowledge - page 39

A few slightly 'adult' jokes - page 45

Storytelling jokes - page 49

A few jokes about other musicians - page 85

"The viola is commonly (with rare exceptions) played by infirm violinists, or by decrepit players of wind instruments who happen to have been acquainted with a string instrument once upon a time."

Richard Wagner, composer

"Viola players were always taken
from among the trash of violinists."

Hector Berlioz, composer

"If you'd heard the violas when I was young, you'd take a bismuth tablet (laxative)."

Sir John Barbirolli, conductor

"All Eric Coates ever wanted to do was to write music to entertain. But for a while he was a professional viola player."

Tim Pollard, presenter on BBC Radio Jersey

"The viola is commonly regarded as of little importance in the musical establishment. The reason may well be that it is often played by persons who are either still beginners in the ensemble or have no particular gifts with which to distinguish themselves on the violin or that the instrument yields all too few advantages to its players, so that able people are not easily persuaded to take it up."

Johann Quantz, composer

A brief history of viola jokes

Every group of human beings, whether a nation, a football team, a profession or anything else, has always had another group it chooses to ridicule and have as the butt for its jokes.

The English, of course, have the Irish, the Americans have the Poles and the Russians have Ukrainians. In rock music it tends to be drummers that come off badly when jokes get told. Medical students mock surgeons. And the list goes on....

In the world of musicians, orchestral musicians at least, it is the viola player who provides the unfortunate stereotypes for numerous jibes and digs about their instrument, their musical ability and, well, about just being a bit dumb!

Bizarrely, it seems that many viola players love the attention that Viola Jokes give to their instrument, their section and, ultimately, to them, believing that such 'joshing" and "banter" is disguised affection or even that it is based on some fom of jealousy.

In my time involved with various orchestras, both conducting and playing tuba, it has even seemed that the keenest to tell a mini-routine of Viola Jokes are actually the viola players themselves despite the jokes relying on suggestions that viola players are incompetent, neurotic and, well, hated, and that their instruments would be better smashed up or burned.

But when did violas become the butt of jokes? - after all, the instrument didn't really exist until the mid-18th Century - which makes it hard to blame Shakespeare but....

Although the main character in Shakespeare's Twelfth Night is called Viola it has nothing to do with the stringed instrument (it comes from the flower which is part of the violet family).

Some, however, have suggested that the character of Andrew Aguecheek in the same play is the victim of one of the earliest ever Viola Jokes because he plays the 'Viol de Gamboys' - this, then, is used by the Bard as part of the character's comic image emphasising his pomposity. This is all well and good, but, of course, the 'Viola da Gamba' (the 'Viol of the Leg') is much more closely related to the 'cello than to any modern-day viola, despite the similarity in its nomenclature.

As you will have seen at the beginning of this book, a number of composers have had really quite scathing about viola players, including Quantz, Berlioz and Wagner. Balancing that, a number of composers have been, at the very least, occasional viola players including Bach, Mozart and Beethoven and it was Berlioz, despite insulting viola players, who, in the 1830s, decided to put the viola both front and centre!

Berlioz maintained that the viola was a beautiful and sorely neglected instrument - it was the people with the bows with whom he had an issue! In a typically romantic outpouring, Hector even called the viola the 'Cinderella of the Orchestra'.

So, when he was commissioned by the violin (and viola) virtuoso **Nicol Paganini**, Berlioz came up with an astounding work of great ingenuity - a programmatic concerto for solo viola and orchestra - Harold in Italy (it was one of my A-level music "set works". The work is based on Lord Byron's epic poem 'Childe Harold's Pilgrimage' and the viola takes on the role of the rather melancholy protagonist who is out of touch with reality. Some have even gone so far as to suggest that Harold in Italy is nothing more than a grand and poorly-disguised viola joke. (In fact, Paganini took one look at the score and stormed off in a huff refusing to play it because it was insufficiently virtuoso).

Nearly a century later, E.M. Forster wrote in his novel A Passage to India about Ronny, for whom image is a priority, but for whom the mention of his viola playing is nothing more than a humiliation and a contradiction to his public persona.

> "Ronny had repressed his mother when she enquired after his viola; a viola was almost a demerit, and certainly not the sort of instrument mentioned in public."

Kingsley Amis wrote Lucky Jim, his first novel, in 1955 and in it he tells of a concert going horribly wrong.

> "There was the most marvellous mix-up in the piece they did just before the interval. The young man playing the viola had the misfortune to turn over two pages at once, and the resulting confusion...my word..."

I feel I should also mention the character of Jake the Dog from the Cartoon Network series Adventure Time which aired between 2010 and 2018. Jake is a shape-shifting dog with a generally laid-back attitude, but who loves adventures and is known to have the occasional fight if it is absolutely necessary. For no reason, other than perhaps comic effect and oddness, Jake the Dog plays the viola - a viola that is home to a worm named Shelby! One of Jake the Dogs' daughters is also called Viola.

So, I'm not sure where the Viola Joke originated, nor really why viola players seem to love them quite as much as they do but, hey, it must be time to read the jokes!

Rob

(Hannah was too busy trying to work out how to open her viola case...)

THE JOKES

1. Jokes about violas

How do you keep your violin from getting stolen?

Put it in a viola case.

What's the difference between a violin and a viola?

1. The viola burns longer.
2. The viola holds more beer.
3. You can tune the violin.

...but why does a viola burn longer than a violin?

Because it's normally still in its case.

What's the difference between
a viola and a coffin?

The coffin has the dead person on the inside.

What's the difference between
a viola and a trampoline?

You take your shoes off to
jump on a trampoline.

What's the difference between
a viola and an onion?

Nobody cries when you slice up a viola.

What's the difference between a dead badger in the road and a crushed viola in the road?

You'll find skid marks on the tarmac before the badger.

Why do so many people take an instant dislike to the viola?

It saves time.

Why shouldn't you drive over a cliff in a car with three violas in it?

You could fit in at least one more.

What is the range of a Viola?

As far as you can kick it.

What's the difference between a chain saw and a viola?

If you absolutely had to, you could use a chain saw in a string quartet.

Why is playing the viola like going for a wee in your pants?

They both give you a nice warm feeling without making any sound.

What do a viola and a lawsuit
have in common?

Everyone is relieved when the case is closed.

Why can't you hear a viola on a digital recording?

Recording technology has reached such an advanced
state that all extraneous noise is eliminated.

Why is viola called "bratsche" in Germany?

It's the sound it makes when you sit on it.

THE JOKES

2. Jokes about viola players

How can you tell when a viola player is playing out of tune?

The bow is moving.

How is lightning like a viola player's fingers?

Neither one strikes in the same place twice.

Why do viola players stand for long periods outside people's houses?

They can't find the key and
don't know when to come in.

What's the difference between a washing machine and a viola player?

Vibrato.

Why do viola players leave their instrument cases on the dashboards of their cars?
1. So they can park in disabled parking places.
2. If someone mistakes them for mafia, they might get some respect.

Why don't viola players play hide and seek?

Because no one will look for them.

Why do viola players smile when they play?

Because ignorance is bliss and
what they don't know can't hurt them.

Why shouldn't viola players
take up mountaineering?

Because if they get lost, it takes ages before anyone
notices they're missing.

If you push a viola player and a soprano over a cliff,
which one would hit the ground first?

1. The viola player. The soprano would have to stop
halfway down to ask directions.
2. Who cares?

A conductor and a viola player are standing in the middle of the road. Which one do you run over first, and why?

The conductor... business before pleasure.

What do a SCUD missile and a viola player have in common?

They're both offensive and inaccurate.

Why are violas so large?

It's an optical illusion - violas aren't large, it's viola players' heads that are so small.

How do you keep a viola player from drowning?

Take your foot off his head.

Did you hear about the
viola player who played in tune?

Neither did I.

Why did the viola player marry
the accordion player?

Upward mobility.

Why can't a viola player play
with a knife in his back?

Because he can't lean back in his chair.

What do you call a bunch of
viola players in a hot tub?

Vegetable soup.

How do you get a violin to sound like a viola?

1. Sit at the back and don't play.
2. Play lots of low wrong notes.

If you get lost travelling in the desert, what do you aim for - a good viola player,
a bad viola player or an oasis?

The bad viola player.
The other two are nothing more than figments of your imagination.

How do you get a dozen
viola players to play in tune?

1. Shoot 11 of them.
2. Shoot all of them.
3. Who wants a dozen viola players?

How many viola players does it take to make a batch of chocolate chip cookies?

10 - one to stir the batter and nine to peel the 'M&Ms'.

Why do you always bury a viola player three feet under?

Because deep down they are all very nice people.

What do you do with a dead viola player?

Move him back a desk.

What's the similarity between the Beatles and an orchestral viola section?

Neither has played together since 1970.

What's the difference between the first and last desk of a viola section?

1. half a bar
2. a semi-tone

What is the main reqirement at the "International Viola Competition?"

Hold the viola from memory.

What's another name for viola auditions?

A scratch lottery.

Why is a viola solo like a bomb?

By the time you hear it, it's too late to do anything about it.

How does a viola player's brain cell die?

Alone.

What do you call a viola player
with two brain cells?

Pregnant.

Why do viola players have pea-sized brains?

Because alcohol has <u>swelled</u> them.

Why do people tremble with fear when someone
comes into a bank
carrying a viola case?

They fear he's carrying a viola
and might be about to use it.

THE JOKES

3. Jokes which might need a little bit of musical knowledge

Conductor: "Let's start three bars before the da capo."
Viola player: "Hang on! We don't have bar numbers."

How do you transcribe a violin piece for viola?

Divide the metronome marking by 2.

How was the canon invented?

Two viola players were trying to play the same passage together.

What's the definiton of "perfect pitch?"

Throwing a viola into a skip

without hitting the rim.

Advert: Established string quartet requires two violinists and a 'cellist.

For sale: Viola, German, 19th century, 405mm. Excellent condition. Recently tuned.

After his retirement, the viola player arrived home carrying his viola case.

His wife saw the case and enquired, "What's that?"

What is the definition of a cluster chord?

A viola section all playing an open C string.

What instrument do viola players envy most?

The harp - it's all pizzicato on open strings.

How do you get a viola player to play a passage both
pianissimo <u>and</u> tremolando?

Mark it "solo."

How do you get a viola section
to play spiccato?

Write "solo" above a semibreve.

What's the definition of a minor second?

Two viola players trying to play in unison.

Did you hear about the viola player who bragged that he could play
hemi-demi-semi-quavers?

The rest of the orchestra didn't believe him, so he proved it by playing one.

What's the most popular recording of the William Walton viola concerto?

Music Minus One

What is the world's longest viola joke?

Harold in Italy

THE JOKES

4. A few slightly 'adult' jokes

Why do viola players get antsy when they see the 'Kama Sutra'?

All those positions!

How many viola players does it take to screw in a light bulb?

None. They're not small enough to fit.

What's the difference between a dressmaker and a viola player?

The dressmaker tucks up the frills.

What is the difference between a
viola player and a prostitute?

1. A prostitute knows more than 2 positions.
2. Prostitutes have a better sense of rhythm.

What is the similarity between
a viola player and a prostitute?

Both are paid to fake climaxes.

Why is a viola solo like premature ejaculation?

Because even when you know it's coming, there's
nothing you can do about it.

THE JOKES

5. Storytelling jokes

The conductor suddenly stopped in the middle of a rehearsal and shouted over to the double basses, "You are out of tune. Check it out, please!"

The principal bassist plucked all four of his strings and then said, "Our tuning is correct - the strings are perfectly tight."

The principal viola player turns around and shouts at the bassist, "Do you know nothing? It's not the tension - the pegs have to be parallel!"

A viola player and a 'cellist were standing on a sinking ship.

"Help!" cried the 'cellist, "I can't swim!"

"Don't worry," said the viola player, "do what I do and just fake it."

A viola player returned home to find her house had burned to the ground.

She approached one of the fire officers to ask what had happened: "Apparently the conductor came to your house, and..."

The viola player's eyes lit up and she interrupted excitedly, "Really? The conductor? He came to my house?"

A viola player decided that they'd had enough of being a viola player. They were fed up being unappreciated and upset by all those silly jokes. So they decided to change instruments.

They went into a shop, and said, "I want to buy a violin."

The man behind the counter looked at him for a moment, and then said, "I'm guessing you're a viola player."

The viola player was astonished, and said, "Well, yes, I am. But how did you know?"

"Well, you see, this is a Fish & Chip shop."

A 'cellist and three viola players were sat together in a restaurant. After a while, a waitress came over to take their orders.

"Good evening," she said to the 'cellist, "are you ready to order?"

"I'd like a rump steak, please. Medium rare," replied the 'cellist.

"Would you like anything with that?"

"What would you suggest?"

"Salad?" suggested the waitress.

"No, thank you," said the cellist.

"Some potatoes?"

"No, thank you."

"And the vegetables?"

"Oh, they'll have what I'm having."

A man went into a novelty shop. He saw an item that caught his fancy - a stuffed rat. He was transfixed by it and enquired how much it cost. "£99.95," came the reply, "but if you buy it, you can't return it for any reason."

The man thought this was a bit odd, but he was so taken by the stuffed rat he bought it.

As he walked along the street carrying the stuffed rat, several live rats started following him. He thought this was rather strange and a bit worrying, but carried on walking.

Very quickly, he had a huge pack of rats all following him and he became quite nervous.

He walked down to the river, and when he got there he threw the stuffed rat into the river. All the live rats that had been following him jumped into the river and drowned.

The man was bewildered and returned to the shop immediately.

As soon as he walked in, the owner said, "I told you you couldn't return that stuffed rat!"

The man said "No! I don't want to return it! I was wondering if you had any stuffed viola players."

A viola player went to a piano recital.

After the performance he went up to the pianist and said, "That was wonderful! I especially enjoyed the last piece you played last... the one that started with that long trill..."

The pianist said, "Uh? I didn't play any pieces that began with trills."

The viola player said, "You know.... [then he hummed the opening of F r Elise.]"

A viola player was crying and screaming at the oboist who was sat directly behind her.

The conductor asked, "Deary me, what are you so upset about?"

The viola player replied, "Just now the oboist reached over and turned one of the pegs on my viola and it's gone all out of tune!"

The conductor asked "I'm sorry, but I think you're overreacting?"

The viola player replied "I'm not overreacting! He won't tell me which one!"

A violinist noticed that at the end of each rehearsal break one of the viola players would look at the inside of his jacket before he sat down to resume rehearsal.

This continued for several months - at the end of each rehearsal break, as he sat down, the viola player looked at the inside of his jacket.

The violinist became quite curious about it.

One day, when the weather was especially warm, the viola player had taken off his jacket and left it on the back of his chair when he went to the loo during the break.

The violinist sneaked over to the jacket, pulled back the flap and saw a little note pinned on the inside.

"Viola left hand, bow right."

An overseas orchestra had just arrived in Europe for a two-week tour. One hour before the opening concert of the tour, the conductor fell ill and was unable to conduct, so the orchestra suddenly had to find a replacement.

The orchestra manager gathered all the musicians together and asked if there was anyone who could step in and conduct. Only one hand went up - one of the back desk viola players.

The manager was very nervous about this. "We haven't got time to audition you," he said.

"No problem," replied the viola player.

"And there's no time to rehearse. You'll have to do the concert cold."

"I know. It'll be all right. Trust me."

The viola player conducted the concert and it was a resounding success.

The conductor was very poorly and remained ill for the duration of the tour so the viola player conducted all of the concerts, receiving standing ovations and getting rave reviews and at each and every venue.

At the first rehearsal after they had returned home the conductor had recovered and took his place on the podim and the viola player returned to his place at the back of the viola section. As the viola player sat down his desk partner asked him, "Where've you been for the last two weeks?"

Once upon a time a viola player was cleaning out his attic and discovered an old oil lamp. He gave it a rub and out popped a genie.

"Thank you for letting me out of my lamp," said the genie. "In return for your kindness, I will grant you three wishes!"

The viola player thought for a few moments and then replied, "Make me a far better musician than I am now."

The genie told him that his wish would be granted. He should to go to sleep and then, in the morning, he would wake up to be a much better musician.

When he woke the following morning he found that he was now the principal viola player in his orchestra.

"Well, this was just marvellous," he thought! But, deep down, he knew he could do better so he rubbed the lamp again, and, once more, out popped the genie.

"You have two more wishes!" the genie said.

"For my second wish, I want you to make me an even better musician than I am now!"

Once again, the genie told him that he should go to bed, and when he woke up he'd find that his wish would have been granted.

When the viola player awoke, he found he was now the principal viola player of a major international touring and recording orchestra.

The viola player was utterly gobsmacked but knew he could still do better.

He rubbed on the lamp again, and, for a third time, the genie appeared.

"I must warn youm" said the genie, "that this is your final wish - use it wisely."

The viola player paused very briefly then said, "I want you to make me an even better musician than you have made me so far!"

As before, he was told to go to sleep.

In the morning, he woke up to find himself back in his original orchestra, sitting on the back desk of the second violins.

A trumpeter in a London orchestra bought an old oil lamp at a garage sale. He took it home, washed it and, unexpectedly, when he rubbed it dry with a tea towel, out popped a genie.

"Thank you, master, for releasing me from my oil lamp prison. I'm sorry, but you have found yourself with a less powerful genie than some, and I am only able grant you one wish - but wish away," said the genie.

"Oh! That's truly wonderful," said the musician, "I think I would like to make a difference in the world with my one wish."

He thought for a moment and then reached for his atlas. "Here's a map of the Middle East. The peoples who live there have been fighting for decades so for my one wish, I would like to to bring peace to this land."

The genie, caught off guard, said "Oh! That's rather a big wish for this little genie. Those people... well, it's all about that religion stuff... the kids begin fighting when they're still just teenagers. I'm afraid you're going to have to change your wish."

"Well, okay." said the trumpeter, somewhat disappointed, "for my one wish, I would just once like to hear my orchestra's viola section play in tune."

The genie thought for a moment and replied: "Um, let me take a look at those maps again."

A viola player was hiking in the foothills of the Alps when he happened upon a shepherd who was busy tending to a large herd of sheep that was grazing in a meadow.

The viola player took a fancy to the sheep, and asked the shepherd, "If I can guess exactly how many sheep you have, can I have one?"

The shepherd thought this was a most odd request, but, because he thought there was very little chance that the viola player would be abe to guess the exact number of sheep he said, "Sure!"

The viola player glanced at the herd, thought for a moment and then made his guess.

"You have 287 sheep." The shepherd was astonished because this was the exact number sheep he had.

The viola player was very excited and asked, "Can I choose my sheep now?" - the shepherd grudgingly agreed.

The viola player chose his sheep, bent over and swung the sheep over his shoulders in order to carry it home with him.

The shepherd then had a brainwave: "If I guess your occupation can I have my sheep back?"

The viola player was a bit surprised, but figured it was unlikely that the shepherd would be able to guess his occupation and so agreed. The shepherd guessed: "You're a viola player, aren't you?"

The viola player was astounded and asked, "How did you know?"

"Put the sheep dog down and then we'll talk about it."

When 'Oetzi the ice mummy' was found in the Alps in September 1991, archeologists and anthropologists were mystified by how he had come to be trapped under a glacier?

Thanks to a joint venture operation by leading music-anthropologists the mystery has found its solution and they released a statement:

"We have decided that 'Oetzi' must have been a viola player - how else could the glacier have caught up with him?"

In order to save money, the musicians of the orchestra decided to build their new rehearsal rooms themselves.

As they got on with the work it became apparent that the hierarchy of the musicians was reflected in the various jobs that they had been allocated.

The viola players found themselves digging at the bottom of a ditch. Above them, in a supervisry role, was a trumpet player.

One viola player turned to another and asked, "How come we're working down here doing all this nasty digging and he's up there lauding it over us?"

The other viola player responded, "I don't know, but I'm to go up there and ask."

The viola player slowly crawled up the steep sides of the ditch all the way to the top.

"Why are we, the viola section, down there digging while you're up here supervising?" the disgruntles viola player asked the trumpeter.

"Because I'm smarter than you," was the somewhat unexpected reply.

"Really? I don't understand," said the confused viola player.

"Please, allow me to demonstrate," said the trumpeter.

He walked over to the nearest tree, placed his hand on the trunk tree and said to the viola player, "Hit my hand!"

The viola player clenched his fist and punched at the trumpeter's hand but, at the last moment, the trumpeter moved his hand out of the way and the viola player's fist smashed against the tree.

"Ow!" screeched the viola player, "Ok, I see what you mean."

Then he returned to the ditch and his fellow viola player who was waiting below.

"Well," said the other viola player, "did you find out why he's up there and we're down here?"

"Yes," said the viola player, his hand was still throbbing in pain, "it's because he's smarter than us."

"I don't understand," said his friend.

"Let me explain," said the viola player.

He took his hand and placed it on his own face.

"Now," he said, "hit my hand with your shovel!"

A group of terrorists hijacked a plane full of viola players. As part of the negotiations the terrorist spoke to ground control and gave their list of demands, adding that if their demands weren't met, they would release one viola player every hour.

There was a groundbreaking, cutting-edge hospital where they they had developed the ability to carry out brain transplants.

A patient asked about the prices.

The surgeon said, "Well, that Ph.D. brain over there costs £10,000. Next to it, there's that brain which used to belong to a NASA rocket scientist and costs £25,000. And that last one over there is a viola player's brain and costs £50,000."

The patient asked, "What? How is that even possible?"

The surgeon replied, "Well, it's in mint condition - totally unused."

Katie was on a longhaul flight so, in order to while away the hours, she decided to strike up a conversation with the person next to her.

"I've got a great viola player joke," she said, "would you like to hear it?"

"I should let you know first that I am a viola player," came the reply.

"That's OK," said Katie, "I'll tell it real slow!"

A psychiatrist walked into a brain shop, and said to the shopkeeper, "Hello, I am here to do some reasearch on human brains. What brains do you currently have in stock?"

"Well," the shopkeeper began, "we have some brains from Cambridge graduates at £10 a kilo. We also have a few brains from Oxford graduates for £100 a kilo. Finally, fresh in today, we have some brains from viola players."

"How much are they?" the psychiatrist asked.

"£1000 a kilo."

"Wow! That seems very expensive! After all every orchestra has viola players. Could you tell me why they so expesive? Are they especially high quality?"

"Well, no, they're about average, but, do you know how many viola players you have to kill to get a kilo of brains?"

One day Jenny came home from school very excited. "Mummy, Mummy, guess what? Today in English I got all the way to the end of the alphabet, and everyone else went wrong around 'P'!"

Her mother said, "That's very good, dear. That's because you're a viola player."

The next day Jenny was even more excited. "Mummy, Mummy, guess what?! Today in maths I counted all the way to ten, but everyone else got messed up around seven!"

"That's very good, dear," her mother replied. "That's because you're a viola player."

On the third day, Jenny was beside herself. "Mummy, Mummy, today we measured ourselves and I'm the tallest one in my class! Is that because I'm a viola player?"

"No, dear," her mother said, "that's because you're 26 years old."

An orchestra was on tour in France.

One evening, they decided they'd like to try to cook up some of the local cuisine, So they went outside to find some snails so they could have escargot for their dinner.

Each musician was given a bag and sent out into the nearby vineyards.

After a while the muscians began to return with their bags filled to the brim with snails.

All sections, that is, except for the viola players, who didn't return for several hours and, when they did, their bags were empty.

The conductor was confused, and asked, "Where have you been for all this time and why are your bags empty?"

"Well," the viola players explained, "We don't know how you all managed, but It was an absolute and unmitigated disaster... we saw loads of snails, but they were so quick! Just as we were near enough to pick them up.... rush...and they were gone!"

Johan went on safari to deepest, darkest Africa as part of a tour group and some local guides.

They did most of their travelling on foot, going deep into the jungle where they were surrounded by the the screeching of birds, the howling of wild cats and a huge wall of sound made by all the other wild animals.

After a few days travelling, Johan began to notice that, in the background, he could hear the sound of drums constantly beating out a rhythm. He asked the leader of the guides about the drumming, but got nothing other than a stony silence in response.

The drumming carried on all day and all night over the following days. In fact, the further they went, deeper and deeper into the jungle, the louder the drumming became.

Again, Johan tried to find out what the drumming was and if it meant something by asking the other local guides, but was still greeted with no answer.

Eventually, after days and days of marching along to the sound of the increasingly ominous drumming, the drums suddenly fell silent.

The local guides all screamed and ran away into the jungle to hide in the undergrowth.

The leader of the guides remained behind with the tour group, but he was sweating and visibly trembling with fear.

Johan tentatively asked "What's wrong? Why have the drums suddenly stopped?"

The leader of the guides replied "Oh, this is very, very bad."

"What can it be?" asked Johan, fearing for his life.

The leader of the guides answered, "When the drum stops it's very bad - next comes the viola solo!"

And, just to balance things up a little....

A few jokes about other musicians...

"Mummy, when I grow up I'd like to be a musician."

"Well honey, you know you can't do both."

ACCORDION PLAYERS...

What's the difference between Terrorists and Accordion players?

Terrorists have sympathizers.

What's the definition of perfect pitch?

When you toss a banjo in the garbage and it hits an accordion.

CLARINETTISTS...

What do clarinetists use for birth control?

Their personalities.

CLASSICAL MUSICIANS...

Why was the classical musician arrested?

She was in treble

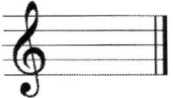

COMPOSERS...

What's the difference between a composer and a large pizza?

A large pizza can feed a family of four.

CONDUCTORS...

How many conductors does it take
to screw in a light bulb?

No one knows, no one ever looks at him.

What's the difference between
a conductor and God?

God doesn't think he's a conductor.

DRUMMERS...

What do you call a drummer
in a 3-piece suit?

"The Defendant"

How many drummers does it take
to change a light bulb?

"Sorry guys, I think I broke it!"

What did the drummer get on his I.Q. Test?

Saliva.

What's the similarity between a drummer and a philosopher?

They both perceive time as an abstract concept.

What is the difference between a drummer and a vacuum cleaner?

You have to plug one of them in before it sucks.

FOLK SINGERS...

How many Folk Singers does it take to change a light bulb?

One to change it and 5 to sing about how good the old one was.

GUITARISTS...

What do call a guitarist without a girlfriend?

Homeless.

OBOISTS...

How do you get an oboist to play A flat?

Take the batteries out of his electronic tuner.

What's the difference between a SCUD missile and a bad oboist?

A bad oboist can kill you.

OPERA SINGERS...

What's the difference between an opera singer and a pit bull?

Lipstick.

PIANISTS...

What do you get when you drop a piano into a mine shaft?

A Flat Miner

TROMBONISTS...

What do you call a beautiful woman on a trombonist's arm?

A tattoo.

What is the dynamic range of a bass trombone?

On and off.

Why do people play trombone?

Because they can't move their fingers and read music at the same time.

What is an alternative name for a trombone?

A wind driven, manually operated, pitch approximator.

TRUMPETERS...

Two trumpeters walked out of a bar...

"Ye, right!"

What's the difference between a jet airplane and a trumpet?

About three decibels.

www.facebook.com/teamhannahrob

Printed in Great Britain
by Amazon